Ourigan, Oregon

I0560139

William Clark,
Richard Robinson,
Anonymous

Sunny Lou Publishing Company
Portland, Oregon, USA
http://www.sunnyloupublishing.com

2nd Edition: March 21, 2024
Original Publication Date: November 12, 2021

ISBN: 978-1-955392-63-1

* * *

Special thanks to Captains Meriwether Lewis and William Clark for their courageous and honorable journey to the West, and for their journals; to Frederick Traugott Pursch for curation of the botanical samples, his excellent drawings, and *Florae Americae Septentrionalis*; finally to President Thomas Jefferson without whom none of that or this would have been possible. May they all rest in peace.

Special thanks to Russell Neville and Travis Papp for their kind obligement reading, and providing feedback on, the *Ourigan* manuscript.

Contents

Foreword

Hearty and healthy, decadent and depraved, old and modern, alternately, all along the Columbia River. It's invigorating, it's discouraging, it's historical, it's fantastical (seemingly), it's botanical, on both sides of the river. It's what made this country great (in part), it's what might bring it to its knees (begging, in oneiric coitus?). A heterogenous collection that either coheres or won't, just like the right and the left, isn't that right?

Kind of like *Parallèlement* in the sense of a dichotomy, and the counteractive but also complementary forces. Some pieces of *Oregon* remind me a lot at times of Verlaine's early poetry, so light and so aery one does not know what's going on (unless one does): don't breathe or cough or it will all disappear. Other pieces remind me of Nerval's *Les Chimères*.

If you like modern poetry, you will hate this collection. That's because it's not the same kind of omphaloskepsis, self-indulgent, self-glorifying "free verse" stuff we see all the time for the last 30 years or more. Because it's not trying to turn every driveling, ho-hum moment into a "poetic experience," nor trying to "meditate." It meditates, but in a kind of out of body experience; it glorifies (maybe, sometimes), but in rhythm and rhyme.

One can be sure that it will never be awarded the Pulitzer Prize for poetry – far from it. For many reasons, which I daren't go into here. Not today, anyways, not the way things are going in the world. You'll need to connect the dots, or row from one bank to the other to see why.

An example of something like early Verlaine is the "Tundra Swans in November" in *Oregon*. And the "Dodecatheon Conjugens" series of poems in *Oregon* are an example of something out of Nerval's *Les Chimères,* "El Desdichado," for instance.

What about the *Ourigan* poems, what are they like? Like something out of Pound's *Cantos*, at times.

The author of *Ourigan* is William Clark, of the Corps of Discovery and of Lewis and Clark fame; that of *Oregon* is an anonymous writer who apparently disappeared into the bush: people are still looking for him (I hope). Has he resurfaced yet? As for myself, I'm the editor.

– Richard Robinson, November 12, 2021

Ourigan

From the Journals of William Clark and Capt. Meriwether Lewis

"Below the Cascades of the Columbia River the Corps of Discovery passed into yet another natural region, the thick rain forest of the Northwest Coast. Many Indian villages dotted the banks of the Columbia, some of them inhabited by people frightened by the coming of strangers. Fortunately the sight of Sacagawea and her baby convinced them that the newcomers were not a war party. Near the mouth of the Willamette River they reentered the world of previously known geography, for boats of George Vancouver's British expedition had penetrated this far up the Columbia in 1792."[1]

---

[1] Gary E. Mouton, Thomas W. Dunlay, eds., *The Definitive Journals of Lewis and Clark, Down the Columbia to Fort Clatsop*, Volume 6 of the Nebraska Edition, (Nebraska: University of Nebraska Press, 1990), p. 1.

Made portage w/ half the Baggage

Made portage 1-1/2 miles with half the Baggage,
Run rapid w/ Canoes without much damage.
Struck a rock & Split, one, 3 others took water.
Meridian altitude 59° 45' 45". 7 Squars Came over

The portage loaded w/ Dried fish & *Beargrass,*
4 men came down in a Canoe. Took brackfast,
Another meridian, & set out again. Passed 2 bad rapids
One at 2, the other at 4 miles below Strawberry Island.

Remarkable high rock on Stard. Side, 800 ft. up,
400 yds round, the natives call it *Beaten* Rock.
Mountains and bottoms thickly covered with timber,
Cottonwood, maple, ash, Spruce pine and alder.

Great numbers of waterfowl of Different variety
Such as Swan, Geese, white brants and grey,
Guls & Pleaver, Ducks, of various kinds:
Labeach killed 14 brants, Collins 1, Fields 3.

The Indians left this morning at portage passed us.
One canoe come up with seven & encamped with us.

– Saturday, November 2, 1805

Fog so thick this morning

Fog so thick this morning, we did not think it prudent
'Til 10 oClock to set out, accompanied by our friends.
Water rose 2 Inches last night, effects of *tide*.
Country has a handsom look, no mountains either side.

Fog continued thick until 12 oClock. Coasted,
& halted, at a large river mouth, on Lard side.
This river throws out emence quantity of sand,
Is verry Shallow, the narrowest part 200 yds wide.

Current bold, Northern banks crowded with sand,
Extensive bottom, low hilley country each side
(Good wintering place). High peaked mountain,
Suppose to be Mt. Hood, at S. 85° E. Lard. Side.

From quick Sand river mouth, a 40 miles ride.
Large Island, at 3 miles, opposite, on Std. Side
Faced with rocks, pine, cottonwood. A large creek falls.
1000 fowls pass o'er head: Geese, brants, guls[2]...

   – Sunday, November 3, 1805

---

[2] Geese, brants, ducks... "Some of the Large and Small kind of Swan, Sand hill Cranes – also luns and White guls."

From the village below the rapids came a canoe

From the village below the rapids came a canoe
Bearing a man, his wife, 3 children and a Squar
Whome the Snake Indians had taken prisoner.
Sent the wife of our interpreter to chat with her

But they could not understand each other much.
That family, & some Indians we met, stayed with us.
Borrowing a small canoe of the Indians, Capt. Lewis
& 4 men visited a small lake in the Island to hunt.

He killed a Swan, making together with the ducks,
Of fowls this evening killed: 3 swan, 8 brant, 5 ducks,
On which we made a sumptious supper.
Gave the Indians a brant, duck meat to the others.

– Sunday, November 3, 1805

Cloudy cool morning, wind from the West

Cloudy cool morning, wind from the West.
One man, Shannon, Set out at ½ past 8 oClock
Early to walk the Island and kill for brackfast
He joined us at the lower point with a Buck.

6 miles long, 3 miles wide, the Island was
Thinly timbered. Tide rose last night 18 in. perpendicular.
At the lowest point of this Dimond island is the head
Of a large island from a small one separated

By a narrow channel. Both situated on Lard side.
Those islands thickly covered in Pine. River is wide,
Country low both sides. Visited a village, 25 houses,
24 thatched with straw, covered with bark, 1 house

Built of split boards, above ground, 50 feet in length.
In front of this village of 200 men, the *Skil-loot*
Nation: 52 canoes on bank. We recognized a man,
Invited us to his lodge, gave us rounded roots

The size of a small potato. He called it Wap-pa-to.
Sa-git ti folia (we believe it is the same), or arrowhead.
Agreeable taste, answers very well in place of bread.
We purchased about 4 bushels of this root.

– Monday, November 4, 1805

We found those fellowes amusing and disagreeable

7 miles below this village, a large island neared:
Saw Elk and Deer tracks; joined Capt. Lewis
For dinner at a place he had landed with his party.
Several canoes of Indians came down and joined us

For purposes of a friendly visit, I suppose.
They had on overalls, shirts, hats, scarlet blankets,
Independent of their usial dress, and Salors jackets;
Carried war axes, spears, sprung bows, quivers

Of arrows, muskets or pistols, tin flasks for powder.
We found those fellowes amusing and disagreeable.
One of them stole my Tomahawk pipe at dinner
Which they smoked with until it disappeared.

I imediately serched every man and their canoes
But could not find my Tomahawk. While I searched,
One Scoundrel stole again, a Cappoe,[3] which
Was found under the root of a tree where they sat.

— *Monday, November 4, 1805*

---

[3] Cappoe: presumably a capote or long, hooded coat.

Sun rose, broke camp

Cloudy this morning, rained all last night
Past 12 oClock. Slept little for the loud sounds of
Swans, Geese, Ducks, Brants grey & white,
On a small sand island. Their noises horrendous.

Sun rose, broke camp, passed 2 houses, Stard. Side.
From up river a canoe come down, w/ 3 men,
Merely to look at us. Passed an island, a short ride,
Large village, 14 houses*[: Quathlapotle nation.]*

Met 4 canoes from below, 26 Indians, of which
One canoe is large, w/ bow and stern ornimented:
A bear on the bow, a man on the stern imaged.
We landed & camped by an Old Village.

Day proved cloudy, rained the vast part of it.
We are all wet, cold, disagreeable. Saw little frost
In the valley we call *Wap-pa-too*, after the plant.
In my walk I saw 17 striped snakes. Killed a grouse.

This is the first night we have been clear of Indians
Since our arrival on the waters of the Columbian.[4]

> *– Tuesday, November 5, 1805*

---

[4] Columbian: the Columbia River, passing through the heart of what was the referred to as Ourigan, and is now the border between Washington and Oregon states.

Particularly fond of a woman in his canoe

Cold wet raney morning. Set out early, proceeded
On course of last night, &c. Bold rockey shore,
Lard. Side, 4 miles in, passed 2 Indian lodges;
Fields & mountains covered w/ pines, *Arbor*

Vitae or white cedar, red Loril, alder, species
Of under groth. Bottoms have rushes, nettles, grass,
Slashey parts, flags & Bull rushes;
Some willows on waters edge. Passed an Island.

2 canoes, w/ Indians in them, goes down river
To trade [w/ Englishmen]; one of them speaks English;
He said, the principal, Mr. Haley, who traded with them,
Was particularly fond of a woman in his canoe.

   – Wednesday, November 6, 1805

Traded fishing hooks for beaver skins

Foggy morning, little rain.
Pushed out at 8 o'clock.
Can't see across river,
The fog is so thick.

Starboard side, steep ascent,
High hill, high land, & rockey.
Two canoes of Indians met us &
Returned us to their village.

Proceeded under starboard shore
Behind a cluster of marshy islands
On a narrow channel to
A village of four houses.

Traded fishing hooks for beaver skins,
And a few Wapato roots.
Old village, seven houses: Bought
3 dogs, berries, salmon trout.

They call themselves War-ci-â-cum.
1-1/2 hour of delay, then set out:
The tide being up &
The river so cut with islands, we got

An Indian to pilot for us.
One of the canoes separated from us
This morning in the fog,
The river very wide in places....

* * *

* * *

* * *

The fog cleared off, –

Great joy in camp.
We are In *View* of the Ocian!
This great Pacific Octean
* * *

Which we been so long anxious to See.
And the roreing or noise made by the waves
Brakeing on the rockey shores...
I Suppose it may be heard distictly.

We made 34 miles to day.
* * *

* * *

* * *

– Thursday, November 7, 1805

The women wear a kind of *Srand*

The women wear a kind of *Srand*,
Made of fur cedar bark,
Soft in place
Of a tight piece of leather

As worn by women above.[5]
Their petticoat is 15 inches long
Made of *arbor vitae,* white cedar,
Bark wove to a String,

Hanging down in *tossles,* tied,
So as to cover from the hips:
Covers them while standing;
In any other position, separates.

   – Thursday, November 7, 1805

---

[5] Above: upriver.

A cloudy morning, some rain

A cloudy morning, some rain.
We did not Set out untill 9 oClock,
Having Changed our Clothing, –
Proceeded on Close under Stard. side.

Hills high with steep ascent,
Shore *boald* and rockey.
Several low Islands in a Deep bend
Or Bay, to Lard. side.

Three Indians in a Canoe overtake us
With Salmon to Sell.
At 3 miles entered a nitch, 6 miles wide,
5 miles deep, w/ Several Creeks,

Found it verry shallow water,
And Called it Shallow Nitch.
We came too the remains of an old village
Lying at the bottom of it...

Saw great number of fowl.
Sent out 2 men and they killed
A Goose, and two *Canves back* Ducks.
Found great numbers of flees....

    – Friday, November 8, 1805

Found the swells or waves so high

Found the swells or waves so high that
We thought it imprudent to continue;
Landed, unloaded, drew up the canoes.
It rained all day at starts and fits.

We are all wet and disagreeable.
Have been for days. Our present
Situation is *verry* disagreeable.
The river is too salt to drink.

Leavel land is scercely sufficient
For encampment and baggage.
To lie clear of tide water, we
Raised the baggage onto wet logs.

Waves increased to such height,
Hills high, so close and steep,
We cannot go back or retreat:
Cannot move from this place.

We are compelled to form our Camp
Between ebb and flood tides.
Seas rolled the canoes all night.
Several in our party are Sea Sick.

– Friday, November 8, 1805

Those monstrous trees

The tide last night obliged us
To unload all Canoes,
One of which Sunk before
3 others was filled with water.

Such emence swells or waves
Added to a hard wind from SW
Loosened Drift trees &
Endangered our canoes. We

Defended them from being crushed.
Those monstrous trees, *maney*
Nearly 200 feet long and
Four to 7 feet through.

　　　– Saturday, November 9, 1805

Nothing to eate but dried Pounded fish

Rained verry hard the greater part of last night,
Continues wet this morning.
The wind has *luled*, the waves not high,
The Swells have fallen,

We loaded our canoes and proceeded
Passed a Deep Bay on Stard. Side which
I call ***. Proceeded on about 10 miles,
Proceeded passed Several deep Small nitch.

Saw a great number of Sea Guls.
Set out in hopes to turn the Point,
And get to better *harber* but
Finding the *waves & Swells* to rage

With great fury, we returned after two miles.
Got a Safe place for our Stores,
Much beter one for the Canoes and
Formed a Campment on Drift logs.

The logs we lie on is
All on flote every high tide.
Rain continud all day.
Nothing to eate but dried Pounded fish.

   – Sunday, November 10, 1805

A hard rain all the last night

A hard rain all the last night
We again get wet
The logs on which we lay was all on float
Wind verry high from SW; blew a Storm

About 12 oClock, 5 Indians come down
In a canoe loaded with fish,
Of Salmon Spes. Called *Red Charr*.
We purchased of those Indians 13 of those fish.

These people are badly Clad,
One dressed in old Salors Jacket and Trouses,
Others in Elk Skin robes. The Wind Shifted,
The Indians left us and Crossed river

Through the highest waves I ever Saw
A Small vestle ride, their Canoe is Small.
Certain it is they are the best canoe navigators
I ever Saw. It rained all day.

   – Monday, November 11, 1805

A Tremendious wind from SW

A Tremendious wind from SW
About 3 oClock this morning,
With hard claps of Thunder, Hail, lightning
Which continued until 6 oClock.

When it became light for a short time
When heavens suddenly became darkened
By a black Cloud from SW
And it rained with great violence until 12 oClock.

A hard wind raised the Seas,
The waves were tremendious brakeing,
With great fury against rocks and trees
On which we encamped.

Our Situation become Seriously dangerous.
Took advantage of a low tide, and
Moved our Camp to a Small wet bottom
At the mouth of a small dank creek.

   – Tuesday, November 12, 1805

I observe great number of Sea guls

I observe great number of Sea guls,
Flying in every direction –
Three men Gibson, Willard, & Bratten
Attempted to descend, in a canoe built

In the Indian fashion, but
They could not proceed, or go on,
The waves tossed them about at will.
They returned after proceeding 1 mile.

– Tuesday, November 12, 1805

Mountains verry high & Pine Spruce

Mountains verry high & Pine Spruce
Verry high and thick
Intollerable thickets of Small Pine,
Arrow wood a groth with briers

Growing 10, 15 feet high interlocking
With each other & Furn;
Aded to this difficulty the hill So steep,
I was obliged to drawing myself up,

In many places, by bowers.
Country Continues thick and *hilley*
As far back as I can See. Some Elk Sign.
It rained all day moderately.

I am wet &c. &c. And saw a Small red Berry[6],
Grows on a stem, 6 or 8 inches from the Ground,
In bunches and great quantities,
On the Mountains; the taste is insiped.

   – Wednesday, November 13, 1805

---

[6] Small red Berry: the "Solomons Seal berry, which the natives call *Sol-me.*"

Wap-to is a excellent root

Wap-to is a excellent root
Roasted and tastes like a potato.
I Cut my hand today.
Dispatched 3 men in a Indian canoe.

– Wednesday, November 13, 1805

Rained all last night without intermission

Rained all last night without intermission
This morning wind blows verry hard:
We can not move, one Canoe is broken,
Waves dashing it against the rocks.

At 10 oClock, 5 Indians come up in a canoe
Thro' emence waves & Swells,
They landed, informed us they Saw
Three men we sent down yesterday.

Soon after those people Came Colter,
One of the 3 men, said he could find no white people
Or Bay; said he saw a good canoe harber, and that
The Indians with us had taken his Gigg, &c.

I called the Squars to give back the gigg:
They would not do it, until a man run up with a gun
As if he intended to shute,
And Colter got back his gigg, &c.

– Thursday, November 14, 1805

The rain continues all day, all wet

The rain continues all day, all wet.
The rain &c. has *distroyed* our robes,
Rotted nearly one half the few Clothes
We got, *perticularley* the leather, –

Fortunately for us no very Cold weather
As yet, for if we have Cold weather,
Before we kill and dress the skins,
The bulk of us will suffer *verry* much.

– Thursday, November 14, 1805

Rained all last night at intervales

Rained all last night at intervales, Sometimes
2 hours. This morning Calm & fair;
I proposed Setting out, ordered Canoes Repared
And loaded. Prepared to Set out, when

The wind Suddenly Sprung up from S.E.,
Blew down the River with Such violence,
Such swells and waves brakeing on the Rocks,
As to render it unsafe to proceed.

I went to the Point in a empty canoe.
And found it unsafe even in a empty *Canoe.*
Rainey weather Continued without longer intermition
Than 2 hours at a time...

Eleven days of rain, Six in this place.
Confined on a tempiest Coast wet
Where we can neither get out, hunt,
Return to a better situation, or proceed on.

The sun shown 'til 1 oClock PM
Afforded us time to dry bedding,
Examine baggage, put arms in order.
Some pounded fish was found spoilt.

At 3 oClock the wind luled, river calmed;
We loaded the canoes in great haste,
Set out from this dismal nitch,
Proceeded on past the blustering Point, below which

I found a butifull Sand beech
With a small marshy bottom for 3 miles
On Stard side, wherein is a deserted village:
36 houses in full possession of fleas.

In full view of the *Ocian* today
From *Point Adams* to Cape Disappointment
I can not see any island in this river mouth
As laid down by Vancouver.[7]

To Point Adams is 35° W 8 miles,
To Cape Disappointment S. 86° W. 14.
4 Indians of *War-ki a cum* nation come down
With pap-pa-too root to Sell us, and –

– Friday, November 15, 1805

---

[7] Editor's note: Vancouver: Captain George Vancouver (AD 1757-1798), British officer explorer, after whom Vancouver Island, B.C. is named, as well as Vancouver, WA (across the river from Portland, Oregon).

The Indians who accompanied Shannon

The Indians who accompanied Shannon,
From the village below, Speak a Different language
Than those above; they call themselves *Chin nook* Indians,
I told them not to steal our gun:

They attempted to Steal 2 guns &c. I told them
If any one of their nation stole anything –
If their womin or bad boys took any thing –
The Sentinel with his gun would Shute them.

– Friday, November 15, 1805

Cool the latter part of last night

Cool the latter part of last night
This morning Clear and butifull
I had, of every description, all our articles
Examined, put out and dried.

The 5 Indian Theves left us. I took
A meridional altitude with Sextn. 50° 36' 15
Which gave for Latitude 49° 19' 11-1/10" North.
Several Indians come up today, I give them smoke.

The Sea is fomeing, looks truly dismal,
Waves breaking with great fury on our beech.
Sent out several hunters and fowlers
In pursute of Elk, Deer, fowls, any species.

The hunters killed 2 deer, 1 crain, 2 ducks
My servant killed 2 geese, 8 brants white w/ black
Wing tips, much larger than the grey brant
Which is one size larger than a duck.

The Countrey on Stard. Side high
Broken, & thickly timbered; on Lard. Side,
At a distance from Point Adams, it is high
Mountains on a Pincal, of which is snow.

– Saturday, November 16, 1805

A fair cool windey morning

A fair cool windey morning, wind from the *East*.
Every tide which rises at this place is 8' 6" &
Comes in with great waves brakeing on the Sand
With great fury, where we lay on the beech.

At half past 1 oClock Capt. Lewis returned
Having travesed Haleys Bay to Cape Disappointment
And the *Sea* coast to the North for some distance.
Several *Chinnook* Indians followed with a present

Of a rute[8], boiled, much resembling Lickorish.
For this root we gave more than double;
Bad practice to receive a present from those Indians:
They are never satisfied for what they get in return,

Even if ten time the value of articles they gave.
This *Chin nook* Nation is about 400 souls,
Inhabid the Countrey on small rivers and ponds
Live principally on fish & roots; kill Elk, Deer, fowl.

I directed all the men who wished to see
More of the main *Ocian,* to prepare themselves to set out
On tomorrow morning.... The Chief of the Chinnooks
& his family came up this evening to see us.

— *Sunday, November 17, 1805*

---

[8] Rute: "cul-wah-mo" in Chinook language, or *Lupius littoralis Dougl.*

I set out at daylight

I set out at daylight with 10 men and my Sevent,
Jos. & Ru. Fields, Serjt. Ordway & Pryor,
Go. Shanon, Shabono, W. Bratting, P. Wiser...
Proceeded on down the shore from the 1st point.

S. 20° W. 4 miles to a rock island in a deep nitch
At the south end of a deep bend where, natives say,
Anchor ships. They receive goods in return for
Peltries, Elk Skins &c. Good harber, large Ships.

Here Capt. Lewis, me & several men marked
Our names, by Land, day of month, and year,
On a tree. From this SW 3 miles to Cape Disapointmt.
Passed a point & 2 Small nitches.

Found a curious flat fish shaped like a turtle,
Fins on each side, *tale* notched like a fish.
This Flownder has a white belly &
Lies flat to the ground. 1-1/2 miles psd. Cape Disapt.

Passed another fish I supposed to be a Grampass –
The men killed 4 brants, and <we> killed 48 pliver,
Two different kinds, yellow & black legs...
Proceeded up above the 2nd point, encamped

On shore, above high tide, evening clear
For a time. Had the kill picked and cooked.
Supped on brant & pounded fish. Men all Chearfull,
Express desire to winter near the falls this winter.

– Monday, November 18, 1805

NW 7 miles to the enterance of a creek

NW 7 miles to the enterance of a creek at a cabin
Or lodge of Chinnooks passing on a wide sand bar,
The bay to my left, to my right: the Mountn;
Several ponds of water fowls in great number

With a narrow bottom of small balsam and alder.
At the cabin, I saw 4 womin and Some Children
One of the women in desperate Situation:
Covered with Sores, Scabs, ulsers.

No doubt effects of venereal disorder
Which Several of this nation have it appears.
* * *
  * * *

This creek a conveyance of several small dreans.
From high hills & ponds on each side near its mouth.
We were set across, all in a Canoe, by 2 Squars.
To each I gav one small hook.

S. 79° W. 5 miles to the mouth of Chin nook river.
Passed a low bluff of small hite at 2 miles
Below which are huts and a beached whale;
Elevated lands covered with pine, thick groth.

The river is 40 yards wide at low tide.
* * *
  * * *
    * * *

– Monday, November 18, 1805

Arose early this morning from under a wet blanket

Arose early this morning from under a wet blanket
Caused by a shower of rain which fell...
Sent two men on ahead with directions to kill
Something for brackfast.

A cloudy rainy day. After drying our blankets,
Set out in direction of the coast
Through emencely bad hills and thickets.
Overtook my men after 3 miles about.

Fields had killed a deer. We built a fire
And cooked it: Sumptious brakefast of Venison
Roasted on Stiks. It commenced & continued
Raining until 11 oClock AM around.

Deer of this Coast differ materially
From our common deer. Much darker, deeper bodied,
Shorter legs, pronged horns, top o' the tail black,
Eyes larger. They do not lope, but jump.

Proceeded on coarse N 20° W from the Cape
Through rugged country of high hills, steep hollers,
To a Point I take the liberty of calling
After my particular friend Capt. Lewis.

– Tuesday, November 19, 1805

Proceeded with my men on up the Beech

Proceeded with my men on up the Beech,
Was overtaken by three Indians –
One of them gave me some dried Sturgeon
And a fiew *wappato* roots each.

Met several parties, on my way up,
Of Chinnooks, which I had not before seen.
They were returning from our camp. All seemed
To know my deturmonation to keep

Every individual of their nation at proper distance.
They were guarded and reserved in my presence.
At camp, I found many Chin nooks with Capt. Lewis
& 2 chiefs: *Con com mo ly* and *Chil-lar-la-wil*.

To whom we gave Medals, to one a flag.
One Indian had on a roab made of Sea Orter
Skins, the fur more butifull than any other
I had ever seen. Both Capt. Lewis & my Self

Offered him many things for his Skins –
A blanket, a coat... all which he refused.
At length we procured it for a belt of Blue Beeds,
Which Shabono's Squar wore about her waste.

   – Wednesday, November 20, 1805

A Cloudy morning, winter approaches

A Cloudy morning, winter approaches.
Great numbers of dark brant pass Southerly
Through the sky, the white[9] yet stationary.
Most of the Chinnook Indians left us.

Wind blew hard. Flood tide raised and dumped
Verry high waves that broke with great violence
Against the shore, throwing water into Camp. –
At 12 oClock, began to rain. From different nations

Or Bands, several Indians visited us today:
The *Chiltz* Nation who reside on the Sea Coast,
The *Clotsops* who reside opposite us on the river.
A Grand rapid chief to whom we gave a Medal.

An old woman & wife to a Chief[10] came,
She brings 6 Squars with her, daughters, nieces,
For gratifying passions of our men. She seems
To view Sensuality <horedom> as Necessary evile.

Received such trinkets for sexual indulgences
As the old woman thought proper to accept of.
Young females, fond of the attention of our men,
Meet sincere approbation of their acquaintances.

The womin all have handsom faces, low bodies
Badly made with large legs and thighs, swelled

---

[9] The white: the white brant.

[10] Wife to a Chief: of the Chinooks.

From stoppage of circulation in the feet
(which are small) by maney strands of beeds

Drawn tight around the leg above the anckle.
Their legs are picked[11] with figures. On the left arm
Of one Squar I saw the letters "J. Bowmon."
All those dekorations as considered handsome.

A woman without them as considered lower Class.
They ware their hair lose, hanging over the back
And Shoulders, blue bleeds in-threaded & passed
Thro different parts of their *ears*, around the neck.

Their dress otherwise like the *Wa ci a cum*:
A short roab & tissue, kind of peticoat
Of Cedar bark, falling down in strings, low behind
The knee, not so low in front. The men have blankets

Of red, blue, spotted cloth, common three
& 2-1/2 point variety; Old Salors Clothes
Which they prise highly. Robes also of Sea Otter,
Beaver, Elk, Deer, fox cat,[12] common in this country,

Which I had never seen before in the U States.
Great numbers of Chinnooks have guns, powder, ball –
The men are low, homely, badly made, with small
Crooked legs, small thighs, large feet.

Both sexes have flattened heads. Maney
Chinnooks have venerious and pustelus disorders.
One women was spread all over in Scabs and ulcers.

---

[11] Picked: tattooed.

[12] Fox cat: Probably the Oregon bobcat, *Lynx rufus fasciatus*.

To each of the men we gave a pece of ribin.

We purchased Cramberies, mats made of rushes,
Roots, salmon, a hat made of Splits & Strong grass,
Small baskets to hold water, made of Split & Straw –
For these articles we gave high prices.

&c., &c.
 * * *
 * * *
 * * *

  – *Thursday, November 21, 1805*

Oregon

For Mei

From the manuscripts of A***

After twenty years of marriage, and a long and bitter divorce in the courts of Oregon, the author of this forgotten volume of naturalistic poetry (written in a beautiful longhand on scraps of loose paper and napkins discovered on the back shelves of a local second-hand bookstore) found himself suddenly without a family, without a place to live, without a means to get around, without much left to go on, financially or emotionally. Two years later, after scrimping and scraping and trying to get by anyways that he could, – after several classes in wilderness survival techniques taken at the local community college – then forcibly unemployed, with very little money in his pockets, and only the clothes on his back and a rucksack thrown over his shoulder, he set out into the backwoods somewhere along the Columbia River Gorge, where he had spent many a day previously in amateur botanizing and lollygagging, when he hoped to clear his head and find his way again, if that were even possible. Nothing has been heard of him since, that we know of, except this.[13]

---

[13] Editor's note: as reported to us by the owner of the bookstore, who requested we not reveal his name other than A***, and which has since gone out of business.

Under the Liriodendron

Under the *liriodendron tulipfera*, at twilight,
Avoiding human beings in Lone Fir Pioneer Cemetery;
General Joseph Lane's Big Leaf Maple in sight,
At arm's length it's not easy to keep society.

To combine nature and artifice is hard.
To hang in a balance, a whirligig of yellow disdain.
An imagined precipice, losing but guarding
One's composure, before the old stone carved fane.

Everyday, to lose one's way, and everyday to walk deeper
Into it. A phone call breaks the silence:
"Where *are* you?" (The wife.) Technology, like a creeper,
Trains its tendrils around our feet with a violence.

– Laurelhurst Neighborhood, Portland, April 2017

Dodecatheon Conjugens

You are gone now, and will I ever see you again?
Red lipped daughter, o *Dodecatheon conjugens*,
Our time together was never meant to be
Long, and now you are gone, away in *,
     faraway from me.

You cannot know the emptiness in my soul:
Where my heart was, now there is a hole.
Meeting again, someday, will you marry me, or will
     you bury me,
As I come or as I go, through the narrow [14]
     Columbia estuary.

— Beaten Rock[15], Columbia River Gorge, June 2018

---

[14] Editor's note: it is not narrow.

[15] *Beaten Rock*: "S. 50° W. 5 miles to a timbered bottom on Lard. Side, passed the Lowr. point of Strawberry Isd. at 3 miles, a Isd Covd with wood below on Stard. Side about 80 feed high and 400 yds round, the *Beaten* Rock. The mountains and bottoms thickly timbered with Pine Spruce Cotton and a kind of maple..." – Captain William Clark, Novr. 2d Saturday, 1805.

Willamette Valley

Winter passes, giving way to another sad year.
Red columbines, manufactured in April, wilt in June.
A peach, culled in June, is buried under roses in
        November.
When seasons cease to follow the mournful tune,
        Children, spread my ashes over the dune.

Stellar jays sport in the bramble, blue and black,
Eastern grey squirrels bury raw walnuts in the ground
While disintegrate in breezes *Camassia quamash* stalks,
A great blue heron quietly wades alone, feet in sand,
        Spearing fish without a sound.

— West of the Cascades, June 2018

The Linden Trees Thick and Strong

The linden trees thick and strong do grow,
Their branches and their leaves grow thick and strong,
They lean down, heavy, down toward the ground.
Riding by them on a bicycle, you must lean down,
Lean down low, or be knocked to the ground.

In the height and heat of summer is a sorrow,
In the evening when the sun is set and sky is blue,
Wispy white clouds glimmer with a silver light.
Then, appearing in the sky is a tumescent gibbous moon,
Where it goes is a mystery, with its silver light.

Early in morning, by the river, where geese do graceful
        glide,
The breeze sets up a thrilling, stirring, vibration in the air.
We sit on the concrete levee, you by my side,
And look out at buildings over the water, where boats ride,
And we feel a thrilling, stirring vibration in the air.

– Portland, July 2018

Tundra Swans in November

On those glaucous sheets of water
Shining yellow black cottonwood[16] leaves,
Falling ever falling[17] to the ground;

On those moving sheets of water
Moving each at different paces and degrees,
Are you at ease, do you feel grounded?

When you stick your head in the water
And pull on a root, or swallow mannagrass,[18]
Can you taste the mountain behind you?

Night falls, you wade in the water
And the last human packs it up and leaves.
When it rains[19], is it all the same to you?

– Steigerwald Lake NWR, Columbia River Gorge,
2018

---

[16] Black cottonwood: *Populus balsamifera ssp. trichocarpa.*

[17] Falling, ever falling: 落落冷澗濱 (杳杳寒山道，落落冷澗濱 － 寒山), Ending, never ending Cold Mountain [path]; falling, ever falling water over chutes. Hanshan (Tang Dynasty).

[18] Mannagrass: Northern mannagrass, *Glyceria borealis.*

[19] When it rains: 夜來風雨聲，花落知多少 (春曉 － 孟浩然), During the night the sound of wind and rain, how many flowers have fallen? "Spring Dusk." Guo Gu Ren Zhuang, alias Meng Jieran (Tang Dynasty).

A Crack in the Sky; On a Path, a Winter Flower

A crack in the sky, snowberries, and a pale yellow aster:
You thought I didn't notice gently when
After it darted out in front of us on the path, a wren,
And you pulled down on, from behind, your black knitted
      sweater.

Months later I look out my window and see
Two silhouettes of two leafless trees, hands raised to stop
Sovereign pedestrians[20]: "you shall not proceed";
A flock of crows caw and defecate from tree tops.

– Smith and Bybee Lakes, Portland, February 2019

---

[20] Sovereign pedestrians: "Chère rappele-toi ce lourd bouque foreign/Que humait goulûment le peuple souvereign" – "Ensense de Foire", *Rimes de Joie*, Théodore Hannon.

The Wetland, Cold and Forlorn

"Souvenir, souvenir, que me veux-tu?"
– "Nevermore," Poèmes saturniens, *Paul Verlaine,*

For a love that was never meant to be,
On a path that was barren, behind a tree
That was leafless, you placed your hand
In mine,[21] O my cousin. The wetland,
Cold and forlorn, now flowered for me,

Larks trilled, and robins animatedly
Encouraged us in a dreamlike felony
That neither of us could countermand
For a love that was never meant to be.

We found a boat and unlatched it, free
On the water that mirrored the sky we
Floated further and farther from land.
Who can reproach, who can reprimand
Us for an act so full of spontaneity,
For a love that was never meant to be.

– Smith and Bybee Lakes, Portland, February, 2019

---

[21] Your hand in mine: "Mets ton front sur mon front et ta main dans ma main" – "Lassitude," *Poèmes saturniens*, Paul Verlaine.

Snow on the Distant Mountains

On the murderous riverine highway there is no time
To enjoy fleeting copses of black cottonwood;
You would be buried between the macadam
And a wide field of grasses where men are fenced out.

There is no time to enjoy Fort Astoria, properly,
Not of a weekend, not of a lifetime. But in retirement, –
Tie your shoe and it's called Fort George suddenly.
The same black shoes they wore in *Dragnet*.

No concupiscence, that Saturday. It was a dream.
A Phoenician sailor, he drowned on The Gallows.
And in the morning, paddled canoe to Washington,
Like Comcomly, a mad escape from white fellows.

A bald eagle solemnly stands on a pile in the river
Looking for salmon in the cold violent water.

– Mouth of the Columbia River, March 2019

Dodecatheon Conjugens 2

Red lipped daughter of the island of my heart,
Our anniversary day is today, on Beaten Rock;
I visited the sacred spot, sacred to my thought,
Where on a path I espied you, and gawked.

Trembling, as I expected, you were not found.
Black sorrowful clouds filled my mind, I thought
My heart was going to break, it made such sounds;
And warm raindrops pattered quietly on fern rot.

Flower of my youth, flower of my depravity!
I dreamed I was a bee, and you compelled me,
Riding the dangerous waves of a riparian breeze
Towards the rock, unsure where you might be.

It's midnight now, in the basement of my middle age,
And a yellow rage blinds my eyes, – my eyes often ache;
I suffer from maculate visions, by Dog River, on tall beds
Near a cabin by the woods, where elk don't tread.

– Beaten Rock, Columbia River Gorge, June 2019

Dodecatheon Conjugens 3

* * *
* * *

There, it's done! You will not blow or bloom
Again before the pedestrian eyes of human scum.

Immaculate calix revealed to me, in pungent form,
You're pressed now 'twixt the leather and horns
Of a Book of Hours, in the bordered illuminations
That hold your flesh in pornographic adulations.

Muse, Danae, receptacle of winter showers!
You might be heaven's queen, but in my bower
You are one thing only: elemental nourishment,
The sacrificial wafer of an eucharistic punishment.

Fair beauty well set! Need I be contrite?
Should your freedom weigh more dearly than my delight?
I'll place you on my tongue where you might melt,
Fleshy calix waver, dying in my mouth, like smelt.

– East of the Cascades, November 2019

Run Leaf, Run River

Run leaf, run river, mend your way south
Fare well, be wary, keep far from the strand,
Go far, be safe, until you reach the mouth
Of the quiet ocean. Do not slacken under aspen,

Tarry under alder shade, find friends among fir
Needles, water beetles, mosquitoes and mites;
From soggy bogs, and dead pools, steer clear:
In solitude is succor, in society despites.

Run leaf, along water, go west toward the sun,
Leave cold and cloud, moss and peat,
Leave shade of ash, and pine of Oregon,
From brook to stream, from stream to rivulet.

Run leaf, move river! mend your way south,
Fare well, be gone: stray not near strand,
Steer clear of shallows; and when you reach the mouth
Of the great Pacific Ocean, pause on sand.

#

American robins, bluebirds, ringneck doves and veery
Maken song all day long in bushes and clearings.
It is hard to ignore, not hard to enjoy. How eery
Time passes, languorously listening to their warblings.

Can you hear the soughing of the breeze in the leaves
Of the red alder, *alnus rubra*, or the Western white pine?

Is that the hand of a shadow of a maple leaf in the sun
That touches your shoulder and makes you freeze?

How far do you expect to get out here?
How long remain? Do you possess the minimalist
Notion of what you can and cannot do out here?
What plans for safe shelter and sustenance?

Evergreen branches for shelter from the rain,
Hemp haberdashery, grasses and cedar chic,
Lomatium dissectum, yampah for stomach "pain",
For a headache, wild spirea will do the trick.

How long have I lived in these back wood?
Beech trunks notched o' steel knife tell the days.
This day on a southern side, I entered the wood
And here, on mossy end, divined wild ways.

# # #

A giggle in the wind, a snicker in the tall thick grass;
The cooing of indigenous doves: a choir for one.
Fresh water from the rivulet, sweeter than raspberries.
The long arms of the fir tree: a roof and an embrace.

These are the best moments! a rare radiant morning, when
        air
Is ponderous, silent and strong, and the sunlight
Beams through branches with unabashed clarity
Breathing confidence into anguished thoughts of night.

Right remarkable is this stillness in the air, ponderous
And thick but also light, pulsing but supine,

Silent but not unbroken by a gaggle of geese, for instance,
Flying overhead, or the crackling of power lines.

These best moments come far and few between,
"Three times a season" – one swag; such satisfactions
That promise great outcomes, act like a hand, unseen,
That pushes gently forward, encouraging actions.

So rare, they must not be squamished.[22] To waste
Them is to give up the ghost without leaving a gift.
The gift, the effort put into the artifact, sheer vestige
Of a life well spent. Rest now, of man bereft.

# # #

The twilight has an urgency about it. The long,
Sidelong beams of sunlight, like inverse directed ropes
Or lassoes fastened around a spider, that wrong
Or right fears the darkness, and gropes to escape.

That time of day when light doth diminish,
And energetic enthusiasms and efforts do flag,
As when the sun like a Sweetgum capsule has
Fallen and rolled out of sight, beyond grey crags.

A man's mind, drowned in a dream, struggles
To awaken, but darkness of day delays all movement,
And dying in his sleep, he leaves behind binoculars,
Botany books, topographical maps, bug repellent.

# # #

---

[22] Squamished: the handwriting on the napkin is hard to read. It may be "squandered."

Run leaf, run river, mend your way south
Fare well, be wary, keep far from the strand,
Go far, be safe, until you reach the mouth
Of the quiet ocean. Do not slacken under aspen...

&c., &c.
  * * *
  * * *
  * * *

    – The Cascades, Columbia River Gorge, 2018-2019

Love, Loving Love

I love to love, loving love! and yet,
Will you love me, love, when I love you yet?
Love, I fear, – love will not love me, but dead,
For alive, love is coy, love loves to love me dead.

But little does it matter to me, in this life, –
Let others bugle, others bray, I care not a whit.
Let them peer at their fingernails, – No matter to me,
I give not a fig for them, they matter not to me.

– Sand River, November 2, 2019

Envoi

Love, love! I want to tell you something,
I wanted to write the novel of your navel,
But I ended up writing the epitaph
Of our ethereal and eternal engagement.

Love, love! I wanted to pullulate Time
And Space with you, to fill horizons
With our seed, and project our Joy,
Fecundating future memories of us. But

Instead, like Pan, among the lonely reeds
I played a sad song, watching the water
Flow downstream, waiting for a moment
When it might reverse course. Alas!

And, like his naughty uncle Bacchus,
Sometimes, I passed out along the banks.
And, like Noah, standing naked in his tent,
I waited for you to cover my nakedness...

But you did not turn.

– Oregon, December 2019

Other Books by the Publisher

Fanchette's Pretty Little Foot by Restif de La Bretonne

Je M'Accuse... by Léon Bloy

My Hospitals & My Prisons by Paul Verlaine

Salvation Through the Jews by Léon Bloy

Words of a Demolitions Contractor by Léon Bloy

Cellulely by Paul Verlaine

Ecclesiastical Laurels by Jacques Rochette de la Morlière

Flowers of Bitumen by Émile Goudeau

Songs for Her & Odes in Her Honor by Paul Verlaine

On Huysmans' Tomb by Léon Bloy

Ten Years a Bohemian by Émile Goudeau

The Soul of Napoleon by Léon Bloy

Blood of the Poor by Léon Bloy

Theresa the Philosopher & The Carmelite Extern Nun by Marquis d'Argens & Anne-Gabriel Meusnier de Querlon

A Platonic Love by Paul Alexis

Two Novellas: Francine Cloarec's Funeral and Benjamin Rozes by Léon Hennique

The Revealer of the Globe: Christopher Columbus & His Future Beatification (Part One) by Léon Bloy

Joan of Arc and Germany by Léon Bloy

Héloïse Pajadou's Calvary by Lucien Descaves

An Immodest Proposal by Dr. Helmut Schleppend

The Pornographer by Restif de La Bretonne

Style (Theory and History) by Ernest Hello

On the Threshold of the Apocalypse: 1913-1915 by Léon Bloy

She Who Weeps (Our Lady of La Salette) by Léon Bloy

The Sylph by Claude Prosper Jolyot de Crébillon (*fils*)

School of Woman by Nicolas Chorier

Voyage in France by a Frenchman by Paul Verlaine